50 Healthy Freezer Meals: Cook Once, Eat Twice

By: Kelly Johnson

Table of Contents

- Turkey and Quinoa Chili
- Vegetable Lentil Soup
- Chicken and Broccoli Stir-Fry
- Beef and Sweet Potato Casserole
- Black Bean Enchiladas
- Spinach and Feta Stuffed Chicken Breasts
- Baked Salmon with Roasted Vegetables
- Turkey Meatballs in Marinara Sauce
- Quinoa and Black Bean Salad
- Chicken Tikka Masala
- Veggie-Packed Tomato Sauce
- Sweet Potato and Chickpea Curry
- Shrimp Fried Rice
- Whole Wheat Pasta Bake with Veggies
- Beef and Vegetable Stew
- Chicken and Wild Rice Soup
- Greek Chicken and Quinoa Bowls
- Stuffed Bell Peppers with Ground Turkey
- Baked Ziti with Spinach
- Vegetable and Bean Chili
- Teriyaki Chicken with Brown Rice
- Lentil and Vegetable Shepherd's Pie
- Zucchini and Corn Fritters
- Healthy Chicken Pot Pie
- Beef Stroganoff with Mushrooms
- Sweet and Spicy Roasted Chickpeas
- Cauliflower and Broccoli Casserole
- Chicken Fajitas with Peppers and Onions
- Spinach and Mushroom Quiche
- Thai Red Curry with Tofu
- Moroccan Chicken with Apricots
- Baked Falafel with Tahini Sauce
- Vegetable Paella
- Garlic Herb Roasted Chicken Thighs
- Pasta Primavera with Whole Wheat Pasta

- Honey Mustard Glazed Salmon
- Barbecue Chicken with Sweet Potatoes
- Creamy Spinach and Artichoke Pasta
- Vegetable Samosas
- Chicken and Black Bean Quesadillas
- Eggplant Parmesan
- Mediterranean Stuffed Eggplant
- Salsa Chicken with Black Beans
- Coconut Curry Lentil Soup
- Italian Sausage and Peppers
- Quinoa Fried Rice
- Chicken and Vegetable Stir-Fry
- Moussaka with Eggplant and Ground Beef
- Thai Peanut Chicken and Noodles
- Vegetable Fried Rice with Tofu

Turkey and Quinoa Chili

Ingredients:

- **1 pound** ground turkey
- **1 cup** cooked quinoa
- **1 onion**, diced
- **2 cloves** garlic, minced
- **1 can (15 oz)** kidney beans, drained and rinsed
- **1 can (15 oz)** black beans, drained and rinsed
- **1 can (14 oz)** diced tomatoes
- **2 tablespoons** chili powder
- **1 teaspoon** cumin
- **Salt and pepper** to taste
- **Fresh cilantro** (for garnish)

Instructions:

1. In a large pot, cook ground turkey until browned. Add onion and garlic, cooking until softened.
2. Stir in cooked quinoa, kidney beans, black beans, diced tomatoes, chili powder, and cumin.
3. Simmer for 20-30 minutes, seasoning with salt and pepper.
4. Serve hot, garnished with fresh cilantro.

Vegetable Lentil Soup

Ingredients:

- **1 tablespoon** olive oil
- **1 onion**, diced
- **2 carrots**, chopped
- **2 celery stalks**, diced
- **3 cloves** garlic, minced
- **1 cup** lentils, rinsed
- **6 cups** vegetable broth
- **1 can (14 oz)** diced tomatoes
- **1 teaspoon** thyme
- **Salt and pepper** to taste
- **Fresh parsley** (for garnish)

Instructions:

1. Heat olive oil in a large pot. Sauté onion, carrots, celery, and garlic until soft.
2. Add lentils, vegetable broth, diced tomatoes, and thyme. Bring to a boil.
3. Reduce heat and simmer for 30-40 minutes, until lentils are tender. Season with salt and pepper.
4. Serve warm, garnished with fresh parsley.

Chicken and Broccoli Stir-Fry

Ingredients:

- **1 pound** chicken breast, sliced
- **2 cups** broccoli florets
- **1 red bell pepper**, sliced
- **2 cloves** garlic, minced
- **1/4 cup** soy sauce
- **2 tablespoons** honey
- **1 tablespoon** sesame oil
- **1 tablespoon** cornstarch mixed with 1/4 cup water

Instructions:

1. In a skillet, heat sesame oil over medium-high heat. Cook chicken until golden brown, then set aside.
2. Add broccoli, bell pepper, and garlic to the skillet, cooking until vegetables are tender.
3. Return chicken to the skillet. Add soy sauce and honey, then stir in cornstarch mixture to thicken.
4. Serve hot over rice.

Beef and Sweet Potato Casserole

Ingredients:

- **1 pound** ground beef
- **2 sweet potatoes**, peeled and diced
- **1 onion**, chopped
- **2 cloves** garlic, minced
- **1 can (14 oz)** diced tomatoes
- **1 teaspoon** thyme
- **Salt and pepper** to taste
- **1/2 cup** shredded cheese (optional)

Instructions:

1. Preheat the oven to 375°F (190°C). Brown ground beef in a skillet, then add onion and garlic, cooking until soft.
2. Stir in sweet potatoes, diced tomatoes, thyme, salt, and pepper. Transfer to a baking dish.
3. Cover and bake for 35-40 minutes, until sweet potatoes are tender. Top with cheese if desired and bake until melted.
4. Let cool slightly before serving.

Black Bean Enchiladas

Ingredients:

- **8 corn tortillas**
- **2 cups** black beans, cooked
- **1 can (14 oz)** enchilada sauce
- **1 cup** shredded cheese
- **1 onion**, diced
- **2 tablespoons** chopped cilantro
- **Salt and pepper** to taste

Instructions:

1. Preheat the oven to 350°F (175°C). Sauté onion until soft, then mix with black beans and cilantro. Season with salt and pepper.
2. Fill tortillas with the bean mixture, rolling each one and placing them in a baking dish.
3. Pour enchilada sauce over the tortillas and top with cheese.
4. Bake for 20-25 minutes, until cheese is melted and bubbly.

Spinach and Feta Stuffed Chicken Breasts

Ingredients:

- **4 chicken breasts**
- **1 cup** fresh spinach, chopped
- **1/2 cup** crumbled feta cheese
- **2 tablespoons** olive oil
- **Salt and pepper** to taste

Instructions:

1. Preheat the oven to 375°F (190°C). Cut a pocket in each chicken breast.
2. Stuff each pocket with spinach and feta cheese, securing with toothpicks if needed.
3. Season with salt and pepper. Heat olive oil in a skillet and sear chicken until browned on both sides.
4. Transfer to a baking dish and bake for 20-25 minutes, until cooked through.

Baked Salmon with Roasted Vegetables

Ingredients:

- **4 salmon fillets**
- **2 cups** assorted vegetables (carrots, bell peppers, zucchini)
- **2 tablespoons** olive oil
- **Salt and pepper** to taste
- **Juice of 1 lemon**

Instructions:

1. Preheat the oven to 400°F (200°C). Place salmon and vegetables on a baking sheet.
2. Drizzle with olive oil, and season with salt, pepper, and lemon juice.
3. Roast for 15-20 minutes, until salmon is cooked through and vegetables are tender.

Turkey Meatballs in Marinara Sauce

Ingredients:

- **1 pound** ground turkey
- **1/4 cup** breadcrumbs
- **1 egg**
- **2 tablespoons** grated Parmesan cheese
- **Salt and pepper** to taste
- **1 jar (24 oz)** marinara sauce
- **Fresh basil** (for garnish)

Instructions:

1. Preheat the oven to 375°F (190°C). In a bowl, mix ground turkey, breadcrumbs, egg, Parmesan, salt, and pepper.
2. Form into meatballs and place on a baking sheet. Bake for 20-25 minutes, until cooked through.
3. Heat marinara sauce in a saucepan, adding meatballs to coat.
4. Serve with pasta or crusty bread, garnished with fresh basil.

Quinoa and Black Bean Salad

Ingredients:

- **1 cup** cooked quinoa
- **1 can (15 oz)** black beans, drained and rinsed
- **1 cup** cherry tomatoes, halved
- **1 red bell pepper**, diced
- **1/4 cup** chopped cilantro
- **Juice of 1 lime**
- **2 tablespoons** olive oil
- **Salt and pepper** to taste

Instructions:

1. In a large bowl, combine cooked quinoa, black beans, cherry tomatoes, bell pepper, and cilantro.
2. Drizzle with lime juice and olive oil, then season with salt and pepper. Toss to coat evenly.
3. Serve chilled or at room temperature.

Chicken Tikka Masala

Ingredients:

- **1 pound** chicken breast, cut into cubes
- **1/2 cup** plain yogurt
- **2 tablespoons** tikka masala paste
- **1 onion**, diced
- **2 cloves** garlic, minced
- **1 can (14 oz)** crushed tomatoes
- **1 cup** heavy cream
- **2 tablespoons** chopped cilantro (for garnish)

Instructions:

1. Marinate chicken in yogurt and tikka masala paste for at least 30 minutes.
2. In a skillet, cook marinated chicken until browned, then set aside. Sauté onion and garlic until soft.
3. Add crushed tomatoes and simmer for 10 minutes. Stir in heavy cream and return chicken to the skillet.
4. Simmer until sauce thickens. Serve hot with rice, garnished with cilantro.

Veggie-Packed Tomato Sauce

Ingredients:

- **2 tablespoons** olive oil
- **1 onion**, diced
- **2 carrots**, grated
- **1 zucchini**, grated
- **3 cloves** garlic, minced
- **1 can (28 oz)** crushed tomatoes
- **1 teaspoon** dried basil
- **Salt and pepper** to taste

Instructions:

1. Heat olive oil in a pot. Sauté onion, carrots, zucchini, and garlic until vegetables are soft.
2. Add crushed tomatoes and dried basil, simmering for 20-30 minutes.
3. Season with salt and pepper. Use as a sauce for pasta or as a base for other dishes.

Sweet Potato and Chickpea Curry

Ingredients:

- **1 tablespoon** olive oil
- **1 onion**, chopped
- **2 sweet potatoes**, peeled and diced
- **1 can (15 oz)** chickpeas, drained and rinsed
- **1 can (14 oz)** coconut milk
- **2 tablespoons** curry paste
- **Fresh spinach** (optional)
- **Salt and pepper** to taste

Instructions:

1. Heat olive oil in a pot. Sauté onion until soft, then add sweet potatoes and curry paste.
2. Pour in coconut milk and bring to a simmer. Add chickpeas and cook until sweet potatoes are tender.
3. Stir in fresh spinach if using, and season with salt and pepper. Serve with rice or naan.

Shrimp Fried Rice

Ingredients:

- **2 tablespoons** vegetable oil
- **1 pound** shrimp, peeled and deveined
- **3 cups** cooked rice
- **1 cup** frozen peas and carrots
- **2 eggs**, beaten
- **2 tablespoons** soy sauce
- **2 green onions**, sliced

Instructions:

1. Heat oil in a wok. Cook shrimp until pink, then set aside.
2. Add cooked rice, peas, and carrots, stirring until heated through. Push to one side and scramble eggs on the other side.
3. Combine everything, adding soy sauce and green onions. Serve hot.

Whole Wheat Pasta Bake with Veggies

Ingredients:

- **12 oz** whole wheat pasta
- **2 cups** mixed vegetables (zucchini, bell peppers, spinach)
- **2 cups** marinara sauce
- **1 cup** shredded mozzarella cheese
- **1/4 cup** grated Parmesan
- **Salt and pepper** to taste

Instructions:

1. Preheat the oven to 375°F (190°C). Cook pasta until al dente, then drain.
2. Toss pasta with mixed vegetables, marinara sauce, and seasonings. Transfer to a baking dish.
3. Top with mozzarella and Parmesan cheese. Bake for 20-25 minutes, until bubbly and golden.

Beef and Vegetable Stew

Ingredients:

- **1 pound** beef stew meat, cubed
- **2 tablespoons** flour
- **2 tablespoons** olive oil
- **1 onion**, chopped
- **3 carrots**, sliced
- **2 potatoes**, diced
- **4 cups** beef broth
- **1 teaspoon** thyme
- **Salt and pepper** to taste

Instructions:

1. Toss beef in flour, then brown in olive oil in a large pot. Remove beef and set aside.
2. Sauté onion, carrots, and potatoes in the pot. Return beef and add beef broth and thyme.
3. Simmer for 1.5-2 hours, until beef is tender. Season with salt and pepper. Serve hot.

Chicken and Wild Rice Soup

Ingredients:

- **1 tablespoon** butter
- **1 onion**, diced
- **2 carrots**, chopped
- **2 celery stalks**, sliced
- **1 pound** chicken breast, cooked and shredded
- **1 cup** wild rice, cooked
- **6 cups** chicken broth
- **1/2 cup** heavy cream
- **Salt and pepper** to taste

Instructions:

1. Melt butter in a large pot. Sauté onion, carrots, and celery until soft.
2. Add shredded chicken, cooked wild rice, and chicken broth. Simmer for 20 minutes.
3. Stir in heavy cream and season with salt and pepper. Serve warm.

Greek Chicken and Quinoa Bowls

Ingredients:

- **1 pound** chicken breast, cubed
- **1/4 cup** olive oil
- **2 tablespoons** lemon juice
- **1 tablespoon** oregano
- **1 cup** cooked quinoa
- **1/2 cup** diced cucumber
- **1/2 cup** cherry tomatoes, halved
- **1/4 cup** crumbled feta
- **Tzatziki sauce** for serving

Instructions:

1. Marinate chicken in olive oil, lemon juice, and oregano for at least 30 minutes. Cook until golden and fully cooked.
2. Assemble bowls with quinoa, cooked chicken, cucumber, tomatoes, and feta. Serve with tzatziki.

Stuffed Bell Peppers with Ground Turkey

Ingredients:

- **4 bell peppers**, halved and seeded
- **1 pound** ground turkey
- **1 cup** cooked rice
- **1 can (15 oz)** diced tomatoes
- **1 teaspoon** garlic powder
- **Salt and pepper** to taste
- **1 cup** shredded cheese

Instructions:

1. Preheat oven to 375°F (190°C). Brown ground turkey in a skillet, then stir in rice, diced tomatoes, garlic powder, salt, and pepper.
2. Stuff bell peppers with turkey mixture. Top with shredded cheese and bake for 25-30 minutes, until peppers are tender.

Baked Ziti with Spinach

Ingredients:

- **12 oz** ziti pasta
- **2 cups** marinara sauce
- **1 cup** ricotta cheese
- **2 cups** shredded mozzarella
- **1 bag** fresh spinach
- **Salt and pepper** to taste

Instructions:

1. Preheat oven to 350°F (175°C). Cook pasta until al dente and drain.
2. In a bowl, combine pasta, marinara sauce, ricotta, mozzarella, and fresh spinach. Season with salt and pepper.
3. Transfer to a baking dish and bake for 20-25 minutes, until bubbly and golden.

Vegetable and Bean Chili

Ingredients:

- **1 tablespoon** olive oil
- **1 onion**, chopped
- **2 bell peppers**, diced
- **1 can (15 oz)** black beans, drained
- **1 can (15 oz)** kidney beans, drained
- **1 can (28 oz)** crushed tomatoes
- **2 tablespoons** chili powder
- **Salt and pepper** to taste

Instructions:

1. Heat olive oil in a large pot. Sauté onion and bell peppers until soft.
2. Add black beans, kidney beans, crushed tomatoes, chili powder, salt, and pepper. Simmer for 30 minutes. Serve hot.

Teriyaki Chicken with Brown Rice

Ingredients:

- **1 pound** chicken breast, sliced
- **1/2 cup** teriyaki sauce
- **2 cups** cooked brown rice
- **1 cup** steamed broccoli
- **1 tablespoon** sesame seeds

Instructions:

1. Cook chicken in a skillet until done, then add teriyaki sauce and simmer for a few minutes.
2. Serve over brown rice, topped with steamed broccoli and sesame seeds.

Lentil and Vegetable Shepherd's Pie

Ingredients:

- **2 cups** cooked lentils
- **1 onion**, chopped
- **2 carrots**, diced
- **1 cup** peas
- **2 tablespoons** tomato paste
- **4 cups** mashed potatoes
- **Salt and pepper** to taste

Instructions:

1. Preheat oven to 375°F (190°C). Sauté onion and carrots until soft. Add cooked lentils, peas, tomato paste, salt, and pepper.
2. Transfer to a baking dish and top with mashed potatoes. Bake for 25-30 minutes, until golden.

Zucchini and Corn Fritters

Ingredients:

- **2 zucchinis**, grated
- **1 cup** corn kernels
- **1/2 cup** flour
- **2 eggs**, beaten
- **Salt and pepper** to taste
- **1/4 cup** chopped green onions

Instructions:

1. Combine grated zucchini, corn, flour, eggs, salt, pepper, and green onions in a bowl.
2. Heat oil in a skillet. Drop spoonfuls of batter and cook until golden on both sides. Serve warm.

Healthy Chicken Pot Pie

Ingredients:

- **1 pound** chicken breast, cooked and shredded
- **2 cups** mixed vegetables (carrots, peas, corn)
- **1 cup** chicken broth
- **1/2 cup** milk
- **2 tablespoons** flour
- **1 pie crust**

Instructions:

1. Preheat oven to 400°F (200°C). In a pot, combine chicken, vegetables, chicken broth, milk, and flour. Cook until thickened.
2. Transfer to a baking dish and top with pie crust. Bake for 25-30 minutes, until crust is golden brown.

Beef Stroganoff with Mushrooms

Ingredients:

- **1 pound** beef sirloin, thinly sliced
- **2 cups** mushrooms, sliced
- **1 onion**, finely chopped
- **1 cup** beef broth
- **1/2 cup** sour cream
- **2 tablespoons** flour
- **Salt and pepper** to taste

Instructions:

1. Sauté beef in a pan until browned. Remove and set aside.
2. Sauté onion and mushrooms until soft. Sprinkle with flour and mix well.
3. Add beef broth, bring to a simmer, and return beef to the pan. Stir in sour cream and season with salt and pepper.

Sweet and Spicy Roasted Chickpeas

Ingredients:

- **1 can (15 oz)** chickpeas, drained and rinsed
- **1 tablespoon** olive oil
- **1 teaspoon** chili powder
- **1 tablespoon** honey
- **Salt** to taste

Instructions:

1. Preheat oven to 400°F (200°C). Toss chickpeas with olive oil, chili powder, honey, and salt.
2. Spread on a baking sheet and roast for 20-25 minutes, until crispy.

Cauliflower and Broccoli Casserole

Ingredients:

- **2 cups** cauliflower florets
- **2 cups** broccoli florets
- **1 cup** shredded cheddar cheese
- **1/2 cup** breadcrumbs
- **1 cup** cream
- **Salt and pepper** to taste

Instructions:

1. Preheat oven to 375°F (190°C). Steam cauliflower and broccoli until tender.
2. Mix with cream, salt, and pepper. Transfer to a baking dish, top with cheese and breadcrumbs, and bake for 20-25 minutes.

Chicken Fajitas with Peppers and Onions

Ingredients:

- **1 pound** chicken breast, sliced
- **1 red bell pepper**, sliced
- **1 green bell pepper**, sliced
- **1 onion**, sliced
- **2 tablespoons** fajita seasoning
- **Tortillas** for serving

Instructions:

1. Sauté chicken, peppers, and onion in a pan with fajita seasoning until chicken is cooked through and vegetables are tender.
2. Serve with warm tortillas and your favorite toppings.

Spinach and Mushroom Quiche

Ingredients:

- **1 pie crust**
- **1 cup** spinach, chopped
- **1 cup** mushrooms, sliced
- **4 eggs**
- **1 cup** milk
- **1/2 cup** shredded cheese
- **Salt and pepper** to taste

Instructions:

1. Preheat oven to 350°F (175°C). Sauté spinach and mushrooms until tender.
2. Whisk eggs, milk, salt, and pepper. Add sautéed veggies and cheese to the pie crust. Pour egg mixture over and bake for 30-35 minutes.

Thai Red Curry with Tofu

Ingredients:

- **1 block** tofu, cubed
- **2 tablespoons** red curry paste
- **1 can (14 oz)** coconut milk
- **1 bell pepper**, sliced
- **1 cup** snap peas
- **Fresh basil** for garnish
- **Rice** for serving

Instructions:

1. Cook tofu in a pan until golden. Add red curry paste and coconut milk, stirring well.
2. Add bell pepper and snap peas, simmering until veggies are tender. Garnish with fresh basil and serve over rice.

Moroccan Chicken with Apricots

Ingredients:

- **1 pound** chicken thighs
- **1 cup** dried apricots, chopped
- **1 onion**, diced
- **1 teaspoon** ground cumin
- **1 teaspoon** ground cinnamon
- **1/2 cup** chicken broth
- **Salt and pepper** to taste

Instructions:

1. Brown chicken thighs in a pan and set aside. Sauté onion until soft, then add cumin, cinnamon, apricots, and chicken broth.
2. Return chicken to the pan and simmer for 20-25 minutes. Season with salt and pepper.

Baked Falafel with Tahini Sauce

Ingredients:

- **1 can (15 oz)** chickpeas, drained
- **1/4 cup** chopped parsley
- **2 cloves** garlic
- **1 teaspoon** cumin
- **2 tablespoons** flour
- **Salt and pepper** to taste
- **Tahini sauce** for serving

Instructions:

1. Preheat oven to 375°F (190°C). Blend chickpeas, parsley, garlic, cumin, flour, salt, and pepper in a food processor until combined.
2. Form into balls, place on a baking sheet, and bake for 20-25 minutes. Serve with tahini sauce.

Vegetable Paella

Ingredients:

- **2 cups** vegetable broth
- **1 cup** short-grain rice
- **1 bell pepper**, diced
- **1 zucchini**, sliced
- **1/2 cup** green peas
- **1 can** diced tomatoes
- **1 teaspoon** smoked paprika
- **Salt and pepper** to taste

Instructions:

1. Sauté bell pepper, zucchini, and peas in a large pan. Add rice and stir to coat.
2. Pour in vegetable broth, diced tomatoes, smoked paprika, salt, and pepper. Simmer until rice is cooked and liquid is absorbed.

Garlic Herb Roasted Chicken Thighs

Ingredients:

- **4 chicken thighs**
- **2 tablespoons** olive oil
- **2 cloves** garlic, minced
- **1 teaspoon** dried thyme
- **1 teaspoon** dried rosemary
- **Salt and pepper** to taste

Instructions:

1. Preheat oven to 400°F (200°C). Rub chicken thighs with olive oil, garlic, thyme, rosemary, salt, and pepper.
2. Place on a baking sheet and roast for 25-30 minutes until golden and cooked through.

Pasta Primavera with Whole Wheat Pasta

Ingredients:

- **1 package** whole wheat pasta
- **1 cup** cherry tomatoes, halved
- **1 cup** broccoli florets
- **1 zucchini**, sliced
- **1/4 cup** grated Parmesan cheese
- **2 tablespoons** olive oil
- **Salt and pepper** to taste

Instructions:

1. Cook pasta according to package instructions. Sauté cherry tomatoes, broccoli, and zucchini in olive oil until tender.
2. Toss with cooked pasta, Parmesan cheese, salt, and pepper.

Honey Mustard Glazed Salmon

Ingredients:

- **4 salmon fillets**
- **2 tablespoons** honey
- **2 tablespoons** Dijon mustard
- **1 teaspoon** soy sauce
- **Salt and pepper** to taste

Instructions:

1. Preheat oven to 375°F (190°C). Mix honey, Dijon mustard, soy sauce, salt, and pepper.
2. Brush over salmon fillets and bake for 15-20 minutes until cooked through and flaky.

Barbecue Chicken with Sweet Potatoes

Ingredients:

- 4 chicken breasts
- **1/2 cup** barbecue sauce
- **2 sweet potatoes**, cubed
- **1 tablespoon** olive oil
- **Salt and pepper** to taste

Instructions:

1. Preheat oven to 400°F (200°C). Toss sweet potatoes with olive oil, salt, and pepper; spread on a baking sheet.
2. Place chicken breasts on the same sheet, brush with barbecue sauce, and bake for 25-30 minutes until cooked.

Creamy Spinach and Artichoke Pasta

Ingredients:

- **1 package** pasta
- **1 cup** fresh spinach, chopped
- **1 can** artichoke hearts, chopped
- **1/2 cup** cream cheese
- **1/4 cup** grated Parmesan cheese
- **Salt and pepper** to taste

Instructions:

1. Cook pasta according to package instructions. In a pan, heat cream cheese until melted, then stir in spinach and artichoke hearts.
2. Mix with cooked pasta, add Parmesan cheese, salt, and pepper.

Vegetable Samosas

Ingredients:

- **2 cups** mashed potatoes
- **1/2 cup** green peas
- **1 teaspoon** curry powder
- **1 package** phyllo dough or wrappers
- **Salt and pepper** to taste
- **Oil** for frying

Instructions:

1. Mix mashed potatoes, green peas, curry powder, salt, and pepper. Fill wrappers with the mixture and seal.
2. Fry in hot oil until golden brown or bake at 375°F (190°C) for 20 minutes.

Chicken and Black Bean Quesadillas

Ingredients:

- **2 cups** cooked chicken, shredded
- **1 can** black beans, drained
- **1 cup** shredded cheese
- **8 tortillas**
- **Salsa** for serving

Instructions:

1. Spread shredded chicken, black beans, and cheese on half of each tortilla. Fold over and cook in a skillet until crispy and cheese is melted.
2. Serve with salsa.

Eggplant Parmesan

Ingredients:

- **For the Eggplant:**
    - 2 medium eggplants, sliced into 1/4-inch rounds
    - Salt (for sweating the eggplant)
    - 1 cup all-purpose flour
    - 3 large eggs
    - 1 cup breadcrumbs (preferably Italian-seasoned)
    - 1/2 cup grated Parmesan cheese
    - Olive oil (for frying)
- **For the Marinara Sauce:**
    - 2 tablespoons olive oil
    - 1 small onion, chopped
    - 3 cloves garlic, minced
    - 1 can (28 ounces) crushed tomatoes
    - 1 teaspoon dried basil
    - 1 teaspoon dried oregano
    - Salt and pepper to taste
    - 1 tablespoon sugar (optional, to balance acidity)
- **For Assembly:**
    - 2 cups shredded mozzarella cheese
    - Fresh basil leaves (for garnish, optional)

Instructions:

1. **Prepare the Eggplant:**
    - Place the sliced eggplant in a colander and sprinkle salt over the layers. Let it sit for about 30 minutes to draw out moisture and bitterness. Rinse and pat dry with paper towels.
2. **Bread the Eggplant:**
    - Set up a breading station: Place flour in one shallow dish, beaten eggs in another, and a mixture of breadcrumbs and grated Parmesan cheese in a third dish.
    - Dip each eggplant slice in flour, shaking off excess, then in the egg, and finally coat with the breadcrumb mixture.
3. **Fry the Eggplant:**

- In a large skillet, heat olive oil over medium heat. Fry the eggplant slices in batches until golden brown, about 3-4 minutes per side. Transfer to paper towels to drain excess oil.
4. **Make the Marinara Sauce:**
    - In a saucepan, heat olive oil over medium heat. Add chopped onion and sauté until translucent. Add minced garlic and cook for 1 minute.
    - Stir in crushed tomatoes, dried basil, dried oregano, salt, pepper, and sugar (if using). Simmer for 15-20 minutes to allow flavors to meld.
5. **Assemble the Eggplant Parmesan:**
    - Preheat the oven to 375°F (190°C). In a 9x13-inch baking dish, spread a layer of marinara sauce on the bottom.
    - Layer half of the fried eggplant slices over the sauce, then top with more sauce and a sprinkle of mozzarella cheese.
    - Repeat the layers with the remaining eggplant, sauce, and finish with the remaining mozzarella cheese on top.
6. **Bake:**
    - Cover the baking dish with aluminum foil and bake for 25 minutes. Remove the foil and bake for an additional 15 minutes, or until the cheese is bubbly and golden.
7. **Serve:**
    - Let the dish cool for a few minutes before serving. Garnish with fresh basil if desired. Enjoy your homemade Eggplant Parmesan!

Mediterranean Stuffed Eggplant

Ingredients:

- 2 medium eggplants
- 1 cup cooked quinoa or couscous
- 1 cup cherry tomatoes, halved
- 1/2 cup Kalamata olives, pitted and chopped
- 1/2 cup feta cheese, crumbled
- 1/4 cup fresh parsley, chopped
- 2 tablespoons olive oil
- 1 teaspoon dried oregano
- Salt and pepper to taste
- Optional: pine nuts or walnuts for topping

Instructions:

1. Preheat your oven to 375°F (190°C).
2. Cut the eggplants in half lengthwise and scoop out the flesh, leaving about 1/2-inch border. Chop the eggplant flesh and set aside.
3. In a skillet, heat olive oil over medium heat. Add chopped eggplant flesh, cherry tomatoes, olives, and oregano. Cook until the eggplant is tender, about 5-7 minutes.
4. In a bowl, combine the cooked quinoa or couscous, sautéed vegetables, feta cheese, parsley, salt, and pepper.
5. Fill each eggplant half with the quinoa mixture and place them in a baking dish. Drizzle with olive oil and top with pine nuts or walnuts if desired.
6. Bake for 25-30 minutes, until the eggplants are tender and the tops are golden.
7. Garnish with additional parsley and enjoy!

Salsa Chicken with Black Beans

Ingredients:

- 4 boneless, skinless chicken breasts
- 1 cup salsa (store-bought or homemade)
- 1 can (15 ounces) black beans, rinsed and drained
- 1 cup corn (frozen or canned)
- 1 teaspoon cumin
- 1 teaspoon chili powder
- 1 cup shredded cheddar cheese
- Salt and pepper to taste
- Optional: chopped cilantro for garnish

Instructions:

1. Preheat your oven to 375°F (190°C).
2. Season the chicken breasts with salt, pepper, cumin, and chili powder.
3. In a baking dish, place the chicken breasts. Pour salsa over the chicken, then add black beans and corn around the chicken.
4. Bake for 25-30 minutes, until the chicken is cooked through and reaches an internal temperature of 165°F (74°C).
5. Remove the dish from the oven, sprinkle shredded cheese over the chicken, and return to the oven for an additional 5 minutes, until the cheese is melted.
6. Garnish with chopped cilantro if desired and serve warm.

Coconut Curry Lentil Soup

Ingredients:

- 1 tablespoon coconut oil
- 1 onion, chopped
- 3 cloves garlic, minced
- 1 tablespoon ginger, minced
- 1 tablespoon curry powder
- 1 teaspoon ground cumin
- 1 cup red lentils, rinsed
- 1 can (14 ounces) coconut milk
- 4 cups vegetable broth or water
- 1 can (14 ounces) diced tomatoes
- 2 cups spinach (fresh or frozen)
- Salt and pepper to taste
- Optional: lime juice and cilantro for garnish

Instructions:

1. In a large pot, heat coconut oil over medium heat. Add onion, garlic, and ginger, and sauté until the onion is translucent, about 5 minutes.
2. Stir in curry powder and cumin, cooking for an additional minute until fragrant.
3. Add rinsed lentils, coconut milk, vegetable broth, and diced tomatoes. Bring to a boil, then reduce heat and simmer for 20-25 minutes, until lentils are tender.
4. Stir in the spinach and cook for another 5 minutes until wilted. Season with salt and pepper to taste.
5. Garnish with lime juice and cilantro if desired, and serve warm.

Italian Sausage and Peppers

Ingredients:

- 1 pound Italian sausage links (sweet or spicy)
- 3 bell peppers (red, yellow, and green), sliced
- 1 large onion, sliced
- 2 tablespoons olive oil
- 3 cloves garlic, minced
- 1 can (14 ounces) diced tomatoes
- 1 teaspoon dried oregano
- Salt and pepper to taste
- Fresh basil for garnish

Instructions:

1. Heat olive oil in a large skillet over medium heat. Add sausages and cook until browned. Remove from the skillet and set aside.
2. In the same skillet, add sliced onions and bell peppers. Sauté until tender, about 5-7 minutes.
3. Add minced garlic, diced tomatoes, dried oregano, salt, and pepper. Simmer for 10 minutes.
4. Return the sausages to the skillet and cook until heated through.
5. Garnish with fresh basil and serve.

Quinoa Fried Rice

Ingredients:

- 1 cup quinoa, cooked and cooled
- 2 tablespoons vegetable oil
- 2 eggs, lightly beaten
- 1 onion, chopped
- 2 cups mixed vegetables (carrots, peas, corn)
- 3 cloves garlic, minced
- 3 tablespoons soy sauce
- 1 tablespoon sesame oil
- Green onions for garnish

Instructions:

1. Heat 1 tablespoon of vegetable oil in a large skillet. Add eggs and scramble until cooked. Remove and set aside.
2. Add the remaining oil to the skillet. Sauté chopped onion until translucent.
3. Add mixed vegetables and garlic, cooking until tender.
4. Stir in cooked quinoa, soy sauce, and sesame oil. Mix well.
5. Add scrambled eggs back to the skillet and combine. Garnish with green onions.

Chicken and Vegetable Stir-Fry

Ingredients:

- 1 pound chicken breast, sliced thinly
- 3 cups mixed vegetables (broccoli, bell peppers, carrots)
- 3 tablespoons soy sauce
- 2 tablespoons hoisin sauce
- 1 tablespoon sesame oil
- 2 cloves garlic, minced
- 1 tablespoon cornstarch mixed with 1/4 cup water
- Vegetable oil for cooking

Instructions:

1. Heat vegetable oil in a large skillet or wok. Add sliced chicken and cook until no longer pink.
2. Add minced garlic and mixed vegetables. Stir-fry until vegetables are crisp-tender.
3. Add soy sauce, hoisin sauce, and sesame oil. Mix well.
4. Stir in the cornstarch mixture and cook until the sauce thickens.
5. Serve hot.

Moussaka with Eggplant and Ground Beef

Ingredients:

- 2 large eggplants, sliced into rounds
- 1 pound ground beef
- 1 onion, chopped
- 2 cloves garlic, minced
- 1 can (14 ounces) diced tomatoes
- 1 teaspoon cinnamon
- 1/2 teaspoon ground nutmeg
- 1/2 cup grated Parmesan cheese
- 2 cups béchamel sauce
- Olive oil, salt, and pepper

Instructions:

1. Preheat oven to 375°F (190°C). Brush eggplant slices with olive oil, season with salt and pepper, and roast until tender.
2. In a skillet, brown ground beef with chopped onion and garlic. Add diced tomatoes, cinnamon, and nutmeg. Simmer for 15 minutes.
3. In a baking dish, layer roasted eggplant slices and beef mixture. Top with béchamel sauce and grated Parmesan.
4. Bake for 30 minutes until golden and bubbly.

Thai Peanut Chicken and Noodles

Ingredients:

- 1 pound chicken breast, sliced
- 8 ounces rice noodles
- 1/2 cup peanut butter
- 1/4 cup soy sauce
- 2 tablespoons rice vinegar
- 2 tablespoons brown sugar
- 1 tablespoon sesame oil
- 2 cups mixed vegetables (carrots, bell peppers, snap peas)
- Chopped peanuts and green onions for garnish

Instructions:

1. Cook rice noodles according to package instructions. Drain and set aside.
2. In a skillet, heat sesame oil and cook sliced chicken until done. Add mixed vegetables and sauté until tender.
3. In a bowl, whisk together peanut butter, soy sauce, rice vinegar, and brown sugar. Pour over the chicken and vegetables.
4. Add cooked noodles and toss to coat. Garnish with chopped peanuts and green onions.

Vegetable Fried Rice with Tofu

Ingredients:

- 1 block firm tofu, pressed and cubed
- 3 cups cooked rice, cooled
- 2 tablespoons vegetable oil
- 1 onion, diced
- 2 cups mixed vegetables (carrots, peas, bell peppers)
- 3 cloves garlic, minced
- 3 tablespoons soy sauce
- 1 tablespoon sesame oil
- Green onions and sesame seeds for garnish

Instructions:

1. Heat vegetable oil in a skillet. Cook tofu cubes until golden and crispy. Remove and set aside.
2. Add diced onion and mixed vegetables to the skillet. Sauté until vegetables are tender.
3. Add minced garlic, cooked rice, soy sauce, and sesame oil. Mix well.
4. Return tofu to the skillet and combine. Garnish with green onions and sesame seeds.

www.ingramcontent.com/pod-product-compliance
Lightning Source LLC
LaVergne TN
LVHW081326060526
838201LV00055B/2477